# 50 Sweet and Savory Recipes for Home

By: Kelly Johnson

# Table of Contents

- Classic Chocolate Chip Cookies
- Lemon Drizzle Cake
- Cinnamon Rolls
- Blueberry Muffins
- Apple Pie
- Red Velvet Cupcakes
- Carrot Cake with Cream Cheese Frosting
- Banana Bread
- Strawberry Shortcake
- Brownies
- Cheesecake
- Chocolate Lava Cakes
- Raspberry Almond Bars
- Peach Cobbler
- Tiramisu
- Pecan Pie
- Gingerbread Cookies
- Vanilla Bean Panna Cotta
- Maple Bacon Donuts
- Key Lime Pie
- Spaghetti Carbonara
- Beef Stroganoff
- Chicken Parmesan
- Thai Green Curry
- Shrimp Scampi
- Veggie Stir-Fry
- Classic Meatloaf
- Creamy Tomato Basil Soup
- BBQ Ribs
- Chicken and Waffles
- Baked Ziti
- Stuffed Bell Peppers

- Fettuccine Alfredo
- Beef Tacos
- Moroccan Tagine
- Chicken Pot Pie
- Stuffed Mushrooms
- Eggplant Parmesan
- Fish Tacos
- Pulled Pork Sandwiches
- Garlic Herb Mashed Potatoes
- Sweet Potato Fries
- Cauliflower Rice
- Crispy Brussels Sprouts
- Quinoa Salad
- Cheesy Broccoli Casserole
- Mediterranean Hummus
- Spicy Black Bean Soup
- Bacon-Wrapped Asparagus
- Roasted Butternut Squash Soup

**Classic Chocolate Chip Cookies**

**Ingredients:**

- 2 1/4 cups all-purpose flour
- 1/2 teaspoon baking soda
- 1/2 teaspoon baking powder
- 1/4 teaspoon salt
- 1/2 cup unsalted butter (room temperature)
- 1/2 cup granulated sugar
- 1 cup packed brown sugar
- 1 large egg
- 1 teaspoon vanilla extract
- 1 1/2 cups semi-sweet chocolate chips

**Instructions:**

1. **Preheat Oven:** Preheat your oven to 350°F (175°C). Line baking sheets with parchment paper or silicone baking mats.
2. **Mix Dry Ingredients:** In a medium bowl, whisk together flour, baking soda, baking powder, and salt. Set aside.
3. **Cream Butter and Sugars:** In a large bowl, use an electric mixer to beat the butter, granulated sugar, and brown sugar until light and fluffy, about 2 minutes.
4. **Add Egg and Vanilla:** Beat in the egg and vanilla extract until combined.
5. **Combine with Dry Ingredients:** Gradually add the dry ingredients to the wet ingredients, mixing just until combined. Be careful not to overmix.
6. **Fold in Chocolate Chips:** Stir in the chocolate chips.
7. **Scoop Dough:** Using a cookie scoop or tablespoon, drop rounded balls of dough onto the prepared baking sheets, spacing them about 2 inches apart.
8. **Bake:** Bake for 10-12 minutes, or until the edges are golden brown. The centers might look slightly undercooked, but they will firm up as they cool.
9. **Cool:** Allow the cookies to cool on the baking sheets for 5 minutes before transferring them to wire racks to cool completely.

Enjoy your homemade classic chocolate chip cookies!

**Lemon Drizzle Cake**

**Ingredients:**

- **For the Cake:**
    - 1 1/2 cups all-purpose flour
    - 1 1/2 teaspoons baking powder
    - 1/2 teaspoon salt
    - 1/2 cup unsalted butter (room temperature)
    - 1 cup granulated sugar
    - 2 large eggs
    - 1/2 cup milk
    - 1/4 cup lemon juice (freshly squeezed)
    - 1 tablespoon lemon zest
- **For the Drizzle:**
    - 1/4 cup lemon juice
    - 1/2 cup granulated sugar

**Instructions:**

1. **Preheat Oven:** Preheat your oven to 350°F (175°C). Grease and flour a loaf pan.
2. **Mix Dry Ingredients:** In a medium bowl, whisk together flour, baking powder, and salt. Set aside.
3. **Cream Butter and Sugar:** In a large bowl, use an electric mixer to cream the butter and sugar until light and fluffy.
4. **Add Eggs:** Beat in the eggs, one at a time, until fully incorporated.
5. **Add Wet Ingredients:** Mix in the milk, lemon juice, and lemon zest.
6. **Combine:** Gradually add the dry ingredients to the wet mixture, mixing just until combined.
7. **Pour and Bake:** Pour the batter into the prepared loaf pan and smooth the top. Bake for 50-60 minutes, or until a toothpick inserted into the center comes out clean.
8. **Prepare Drizzle:** While the cake is baking, combine the lemon juice and sugar for the drizzle in a small bowl.
9. **Drizzle:** Once the cake is done and slightly cooled, pierce it with a toothpick and pour the lemon drizzle evenly over the top. Let it soak in and cool completely before serving.

Enjoy your tangy and sweet Lemon Drizzle Cake!

**Cinnamon Rolls**

**Ingredients:**

- **For the Dough:**
    - 1 cup warm milk (110°F/45°C)
    - 1/4 cup granulated sugar
    - 2 1/4 teaspoons active dry yeast
    - 1/4 cup unsalted butter (melted)
    - 1 large egg
    - 3 1/2 to 4 cups all-purpose flour
    - 1/2 teaspoon salt
- **For the Filling:**
    - 1/2 cup unsalted butter (softened)
    - 1 cup brown sugar (packed)
    - 2 tablespoons ground cinnamon
- **For the Glaze:**
    - 1 cup powdered sugar
    - 2 tablespoons milk
    - 1/2 teaspoon vanilla extract

**Instructions:**

1. **Activate Yeast:** In a small bowl, mix warm milk and sugar. Sprinkle yeast over the top and let it sit for 5 minutes until frothy.
2. **Prepare Dough:** In a large bowl, combine yeast mixture, melted butter, and egg. Add 3 1/2 cups flour and salt. Mix until a dough forms. Knead on a floured surface for 5-7 minutes until smooth and elastic, adding more flour if necessary.
3. **Rise:** Place dough in a greased bowl, cover, and let rise in a warm place for 1 hour, or until doubled in size.
4. **Prepare Filling:** Mix softened butter, brown sugar, and cinnamon in a bowl.
5. **Roll Out Dough:** Punch down dough and roll it out into a rectangle (about 12x18 inches) on a floured surface.
6. **Add Filling:** Spread the cinnamon mixture evenly over the dough.
7. **Roll and Slice:** Roll the dough tightly into a log and cut into 12 slices. Place slices in a greased baking dish.
8. **Second Rise:** Cover and let rise for 30 minutes, or until doubled.
9. **Bake:** Preheat oven to 350°F (175°C). Bake for 20-25 minutes, or until golden brown.
10. **Prepare Glaze:** While rolls are baking, mix powdered sugar, milk, and vanilla until smooth.
11. **Glaze Rolls:** Drizzle the glaze over the warm rolls once they come out of the oven.

Enjoy your soft and gooey cinnamon rolls!

**Blueberry Muffins**

**Ingredients:**

- **For the Muffins:**
    - 1 1/2 cups all-purpose flour
    - 1/2 cup granulated sugar
    - 1/4 cup packed brown sugar
    - 2 teaspoons baking powder
    - 1/2 teaspoon salt
    - 1/2 cup unsalted butter (melted and cooled)
    - 1/2 cup milk
    - 2 large eggs
    - 1 teaspoon vanilla extract
    - 1 1/2 cups fresh or frozen blueberries (if using frozen, do not thaw)
- **For the Topping (optional):**
    - 2 tablespoons granulated sugar
    - 1/2 teaspoon ground cinnamon

**Instructions:**

1. **Preheat Oven:** Preheat your oven to 375°F (190°C). Line a muffin tin with paper liners or lightly grease it.
2. **Mix Dry Ingredients:** In a large bowl, whisk together flour, granulated sugar, brown sugar, baking powder, and salt.
3. **Combine Wet Ingredients:** In a separate bowl, mix together melted butter, milk, eggs, and vanilla extract.
4. **Combine Wet and Dry Ingredients:** Pour the wet ingredients into the dry ingredients and stir until just combined. Be careful not to overmix.
5. **Fold in Blueberries:** Gently fold in the blueberries.
6. **Scoop Batter:** Divide the batter evenly among the muffin cups, filling each about 2/3 full.
7. **Prepare Topping (optional):** In a small bowl, mix granulated sugar and cinnamon. Sprinkle the mixture over the tops of the muffins.
8. **Bake:** Bake for 20-25 minutes, or until a toothpick inserted into the center of a muffin comes out clean and the tops are golden brown.
9. **Cool:** Allow the muffins to cool in the tin for 5 minutes, then transfer them to a wire rack to cool completely.

Enjoy your fresh and delicious blueberry muffins!

**Apple Pie**

**Ingredients:**

- **For the Pie Crust:**
    - 2 1/2 cups all-purpose flour
    - 1 cup unsalted butter (cold, cut into cubes)
    - 1/4 cup granulated sugar
    - 1/4 teaspoon salt
    - 6-8 tablespoons ice water
- **For the Filling:**
    - 6 cups peeled, cored, and sliced apples (such as Granny Smith or Honeycrisp)
    - 3/4 cup granulated sugar
    - 1/4 cup brown sugar
    - 1/4 cup all-purpose flour
    - 1 teaspoon ground cinnamon
    - 1/4 teaspoon ground nutmeg
    - 1 tablespoon lemon juice
- **For the Egg Wash:**
    - 1 egg (beaten)
    - 1 tablespoon milk
    - Granulated sugar for sprinkling (optional)

**Instructions:**

1. **Prepare Pie Crust:** In a large bowl, mix flour, sugar, and salt. Cut in butter with a pastry cutter or your fingers until the mixture resembles coarse crumbs. Gradually add ice water, stirring until the dough begins to come together. Divide dough into two discs, wrap in plastic, and refrigerate for at least 1 hour.
2. **Prepare Filling:** In a large bowl, combine sliced apples, granulated sugar, brown sugar, flour, cinnamon, nutmeg, and lemon juice. Set aside.
3. **Roll Out Dough:** On a floured surface, roll out one dough disc to fit a 9-inch pie pan. Transfer to the pan and trim edges.
4. **Add Filling:** Pour the apple mixture into the pie crust.
5. **Top Pie:** Roll out the second dough disc and place over the filling. Trim and crimp the edges to seal. Cut slits in the top crust to allow steam to escape. Brush with the egg wash and sprinkle with granulated sugar if desired.
6. **Bake:** Preheat oven to 425°F (220°C). Bake for 45-55 minutes, or until the crust is golden brown and the filling is bubbly. If the edges brown too quickly, cover them with foil.
7. **Cool:** Let the pie cool on a wire rack for at least 2 hours before serving to allow the filling to set.

Enjoy your homemade apple pie!

**Red Velvet Cupcakes**

**Ingredients:**

- **For the Cupcakes:**
    - 1 1/2 cups all-purpose flour
    - 1 cup granulated sugar
    - 1/2 teaspoon baking soda
    - 1/2 teaspoon baking powder
    - 1/2 teaspoon salt
    - 1 cup vegetable oil
    - 1/2 cup buttermilk
    - 1 large egg
    - 2 tablespoons cocoa powder
    - 2 tablespoons red food coloring
    - 1 teaspoon vanilla extract
    - 1 teaspoon white vinegar
- **For the Cream Cheese Frosting:**
    - 8 oz (225g) cream cheese (softened)
    - 1/2 cup unsalted butter (softened)
    - 4 cups powdered sugar
    - 1 teaspoon vanilla extract

**Instructions:**

1. **Preheat Oven:** Preheat your oven to 350°F (175°C). Line a muffin tin with paper liners.
2. **Mix Dry Ingredients:** In a medium bowl, whisk together flour, sugar, baking soda, baking powder, and salt.
3. **Combine Wet Ingredients:** In another bowl, mix oil, buttermilk, egg, cocoa powder, red food coloring, vanilla extract, and vinegar.
4. **Combine Mixtures:** Gradually add the dry ingredients to the wet ingredients, mixing just until combined.
5. **Fill Cupcake Liners:** Divide the batter evenly among the cupcake liners, filling each about 2/3 full.
6. **Bake:** Bake for 18-20 minutes, or until a toothpick inserted into the center comes out clean. Allow to cool in the tin for 5 minutes before transferring to a wire rack to cool completely.
7. **Prepare Frosting:** In a bowl, beat together the cream cheese and butter until smooth. Gradually add powdered sugar and vanilla, and beat until fluffy.
8. **Frost Cupcakes:** Once cupcakes are completely cool, frost with cream cheese frosting.

Enjoy your delightful Red Velvet Cupcakes!

**Carrot Cake with Cream Cheese Frosting**

**Ingredients:**

- **For the Cake:**
    - 1 1/2 cups all-purpose flour
    - 1 cup granulated sugar
    - 1/2 cup packed brown sugar
    - 1 teaspoon baking powder
    - 1/2 teaspoon baking soda
    - 1/2 teaspoon salt
    - 1 teaspoon ground cinnamon
    - 1/2 teaspoon ground nutmeg
    - 1/2 teaspoon ground ginger
    - 1/2 cup vegetable oil
    - 4 large eggs
    - 2 cups finely grated carrots (about 4 medium carrots)
    - 1/2 cup crushed pineapple (drained)
    - 1/2 cup chopped walnuts or pecans (optional)
    - 1/2 cup raisins (optional)
- **For the Cream Cheese Frosting:**
    - 8 oz (225g) cream cheese (softened)
    - 1/2 cup unsalted butter (softened)
    - 4 cups powdered sugar
    - 1 teaspoon vanilla extract

**Instructions:**

1. **Preheat Oven:** Preheat your oven to 350°F (175°C). Grease and flour two 9-inch round cake pans.
2. **Mix Dry Ingredients:** In a medium bowl, whisk together flour, granulated sugar, brown sugar, baking powder, baking soda, salt, cinnamon, nutmeg, and ginger.
3. **Combine Wet Ingredients:** In a large bowl, whisk together oil and eggs until well combined. Stir in grated carrots, pineapple, walnuts, and raisins.
4. **Combine Mixtures:** Gradually add dry ingredients to the wet ingredients, mixing until just combined.
5. **Pour and Bake:** Divide the batter evenly between the prepared pans. Bake for 30-35 minutes, or until a toothpick inserted into the center comes out clean. Allow cakes to cool in pans for 10 minutes, then transfer to a wire rack to cool completely.
6. **Prepare Frosting:** In a bowl, beat cream cheese and butter until smooth. Gradually add powdered sugar and vanilla, and beat until creamy.
7. **Frost Cake:** Once cakes are completely cool, frost with cream cheese frosting.

Enjoy your moist and flavorful carrot cake!

**Banana Bread**

**Ingredients:**

- 1 1/2 cups all-purpose flour
- 1 teaspoon baking powder
- 1/2 teaspoon baking soda
- 1/4 teaspoon salt
- 1/2 cup unsalted butter (room temperature)
- 1 cup granulated sugar
- 2 large eggs
- 1 cup mashed ripe bananas (about 2-3 bananas)
- 1 teaspoon vanilla extract
- Optional: 1/2 cup chopped walnuts or chocolate chips

**Instructions:**

1. **Preheat Oven:** Preheat your oven to 350°F (175°C). Grease a 9x5-inch loaf pan.
2. **Mix Dry Ingredients:** In a medium bowl, whisk together flour, baking powder, baking soda, and salt.
3. **Cream Butter and Sugar:** In a large bowl, beat the butter and sugar until light and fluffy.
4. **Add Eggs and Bananas:** Beat in the eggs, one at a time, then stir in the mashed bananas and vanilla extract.
5. **Combine Mixtures:** Gradually add the dry ingredients to the wet ingredients, mixing just until combined. Fold in nuts or chocolate chips if using.
6. **Pour and Bake:** Pour the batter into the prepared loaf pan. Bake for 60-70 minutes, or until a toothpick inserted into the center comes out clean.
7. **Cool:** Let the bread cool in the pan for 10 minutes before transferring to a wire rack to cool completely.

Enjoy your homemade banana bread!

# Strawberry Shortcake

**Ingredients:**

- **For the Shortcakes:**
    - 2 cups all-purpose flour
    - 1/4 cup granulated sugar
    - 1 tablespoon baking powder
    - 1/2 teaspoon salt
    - 1/2 cup unsalted butter (cold, cut into small pieces)
    - 2/3 cup milk
    - 1 teaspoon vanilla extract
- **For the Strawberries:**
    - 4 cups fresh strawberries (sliced)
    - 1/4 cup granulated sugar
    - 1 tablespoon lemon juice (optional)
- **For the Whipped Cream:**
    - 1 cup heavy cream
    - 2 tablespoons powdered sugar
    - 1 teaspoon vanilla extract

**Instructions:**

1. **Prepare Strawberries:** In a medium bowl, toss the sliced strawberries with granulated sugar and lemon juice (if using). Let them sit for at least 30 minutes to macerate and release their juices.
2. **Preheat Oven:** Preheat your oven to 425°F (220°C). Line a baking sheet with parchment paper.
3. **Mix Dry Ingredients:** In a large bowl, whisk together flour, sugar, baking powder, and salt.
4. **Cut in Butter:** Add the cold butter to the dry ingredients. Use a pastry cutter or your fingers to cut the butter into the flour mixture until it resembles coarse crumbs.
5. **Add Wet Ingredients:** Stir in the milk and vanilla extract until just combined. The dough will be somewhat sticky.
6. **Shape Shortcakes:** Turn the dough out onto a floured surface and gently pat it into a rectangle about 1-inch thick. Use a round cutter or a glass to cut out shortcakes. Re-roll the dough scraps if necessary to cut out additional shortcakes.
7. **Bake:** Place the shortcakes on the prepared baking sheet. Bake for 12-15 minutes, or until golden brown. Allow to cool slightly.
8. **Prepare Whipped Cream:** While the shortcakes are baking, beat the heavy cream, powdered sugar, and vanilla extract in a bowl with an electric mixer until stiff peaks form.

9. **Assemble:** Slice the shortcakes in half horizontally. Spoon a generous amount of macerated strawberries over the bottom half, then top with a dollop of whipped cream. Place the top half of the shortcake on top.

Enjoy your delicious and classic Strawberry Shortcake!

**Brownies**

**Ingredients:**

- 1/2 cup (1 stick) unsalted butter
- 1 cup granulated sugar
- 2 large eggs
- 1 teaspoon vanilla extract
- 1/3 cup unsweetened cocoa powder
- 1/2 cup all-purpose flour
- 1/4 teaspoon salt
- 1/4 teaspoon baking powder
- Optional: 1/2 cup chocolate chips or chopped nuts

**Instructions:**

1. **Preheat Oven:** Preheat your oven to 350°F (175°C). Grease or line an 8x8-inch baking pan with parchment paper.
2. **Melt Butter:** In a medium saucepan, melt the butter over low heat. Remove from heat and stir in the granulated sugar, eggs, and vanilla extract.
3. **Combine Dry Ingredients:** In a separate bowl, whisk together cocoa powder, flour, salt, and baking powder.
4. **Mix Together:** Stir the dry ingredients into the butter mixture until well combined. If using, fold in chocolate chips or nuts.
5. **Pour and Bake:** Spread the batter evenly in the prepared pan. Bake for 20-25 minutes, or until a toothpick inserted into the center comes out with a few moist crumbs.
6. **Cool:** Let the brownies cool in the pan on a wire rack before cutting into squares.

Enjoy your rich and decadent brownies!

**Cheesecake**

**Ingredients:**

- **For the Crust:**
    - 1 1/2 cups graham cracker crumbs
    - 1/4 cup granulated sugar
    - 1/2 cup unsalted butter (melted)
- **For the Filling:**
    - 4 (8 oz) packages cream cheese (softened)
    - 1 cup granulated sugar
    - 1 teaspoon vanilla extract
    - 4 large eggs
    - 1 cup sour cream
    - 1 cup heavy cream
- **For the Topping (optional):**
    - Fresh fruit or fruit compote
    - Whipped cream

**Instructions:**

1. **Preheat Oven:** Preheat your oven to 325°F (160°C). Grease a 9-inch springform pan.
2. **Prepare Crust:** In a medium bowl, combine graham cracker crumbs, sugar, and melted butter. Press the mixture into the bottom of the prepared pan. Bake for 10 minutes, then let cool.
3. **Prepare Filling:** In a large bowl, beat cream cheese until smooth. Add sugar and vanilla extract, and beat until well combined. Add eggs one at a time, beating on low speed after each addition. Mix in sour cream and heavy cream until smooth.
4. **Pour Filling:** Pour the filling over the cooled crust.
5. **Bake:** Bake for 60-70 minutes, or until the center is set and the edges are lightly golden. Turn off the oven and let the cheesecake cool in the oven with the door slightly open for 1 hour.
6. **Chill:** Refrigerate the cheesecake for at least 4 hours, or overnight for best results.
7. **Top and Serve:** Before serving, top with fresh fruit, fruit compote, or whipped cream if desired.

Enjoy your rich and creamy cheesecake!

**Chocolate Lava Cakes**

**Ingredients:**

- 1/2 cup (1 stick) unsalted butter
- 1 cup semi-sweet chocolate chips or chopped chocolate
- 1 cup powdered sugar
- 2 large eggs
- 2 large egg yolks
- 1 teaspoon vanilla extract
- 1/2 cup all-purpose flour
- A pinch of salt
- Optional: Butter and cocoa powder for greasing ramekins

**Instructions:**

1. **Preheat Oven:** Preheat your oven to 425°F (220°C). Grease 4 ramekins with butter and dust with cocoa powder if desired.
2. **Melt Chocolate and Butter:** In a medium saucepan, melt butter and chocolate together over low heat, stirring until smooth. Remove from heat and stir in powdered sugar.
3. **Add Eggs:** Whisk in the eggs, egg yolks, and vanilla extract until well combined.
4. **Add Flour:** Stir in flour and salt until just combined. The batter will be thick.
5. **Pour and Bake:** Divide the batter evenly among the prepared ramekins. Bake for 12-14 minutes, or until the edges are firm but the centers are still soft.
6. **Cool and Serve:** Let the cakes cool in the ramekins for 1 minute. Run a knife around the edges to loosen, then invert onto plates. Serve immediately, ideally with a scoop of vanilla ice cream or a dollop of whipped cream.

Enjoy your gooey, chocolatey lava cakes!

**Raspberry Almond Bars**

**Ingredients:**

- **For the Crust and Topping:**
    - 1 1/2 cups all-purpose flour
    - 1/2 cup granulated sugar
    - 1/2 cup unsalted butter (cold, cut into cubes)
    - 1/2 teaspoon almond extract
    - 1/2 cup sliced almonds
- **For the Filling:**
    - 1 cup raspberry jam or preserves
    - 1 tablespoon lemon juice (optional, for extra zing)

**Instructions:**

1. **Preheat Oven:** Preheat your oven to 350°F (175°C). Grease or line an 8x8-inch baking pan with parchment paper.
2. **Prepare Crust:** In a medium bowl, combine flour and sugar. Cut in the cold butter using a pastry cutter or your fingers until the mixture resembles coarse crumbs. Stir in almond extract.
3. **Press and Bake:** Press half of the crumb mixture evenly into the bottom of the prepared pan. Bake for 10 minutes, then remove from oven.
4. **Add Filling:** Spread raspberry jam evenly over the partially baked crust. If using lemon juice, mix it into the jam before spreading.
5. **Add Topping:** Sprinkle the remaining crumb mixture evenly over the raspberry layer. Sprinkle sliced almonds on top.
6. **Bake:** Bake for an additional 25-30 minutes, or until the topping is golden brown.
7. **Cool and Cut:** Let the bars cool completely in the pan before cutting into squares.

Enjoy your delicious Raspberry Almond Bars!

**Peach Cobbler**

**Ingredients:**

- **For the Filling:**
    - 6 cups fresh peaches (peeled, pitted, and sliced) or 4 cups canned peaches (drained)
    - 1 cup granulated sugar
    - 1/4 cup brown sugar
    - 1/4 cup cornstarch
    - 1 teaspoon ground cinnamon
    - 1/4 teaspoon ground nutmeg
    - 1 tablespoon lemon juice
- **For the Topping:**
    - 1 1/2 cups all-purpose flour
    - 1/4 cup granulated sugar
    - 1/4 cup brown sugar
    - 2 teaspoons baking powder
    - 1/2 teaspoon salt
    - 1/2 cup unsalted butter (cold and cubed)
    - 3/4 cup milk

**Instructions:**

1. **Preheat Oven:** Preheat your oven to 375°F (190°C).
2. **Prepare Filling:** In a large bowl, toss the peaches with granulated sugar, brown sugar, cornstarch, cinnamon, nutmeg, and lemon juice. Pour the peach mixture into a 9x13-inch baking dish.
3. **Prepare Topping:** In a medium bowl, whisk together flour, granulated sugar, brown sugar, baking powder, and salt. Cut in the cold butter with a pastry cutter or your fingers until the mixture resembles coarse crumbs. Stir in the milk until just combined.
4. **Add Topping:** Drop spoonfuls of the topping over the peach filling, spreading it out as best as you can.
5. **Bake:** Bake for 40-45 minutes, or until the topping is golden brown and the filling is bubbly.
6. **Cool:** Allow the cobbler to cool slightly before serving. It can be enjoyed warm, ideally with a scoop of vanilla ice cream or a dollop of whipped cream.

Enjoy your delicious Peach Cobbler!

# Tiramisu

**Ingredients:**

- **For the Mascarpone Mixture:**
    - 6 large egg yolks
    - 3/4 cup granulated sugar
    - 1 cup heavy cream
    - 1 pound (16 oz) mascarpone cheese (room temperature)
    - 1 teaspoon vanilla extract
- **For the Coffee Mixture:**
    - 1 cup brewed espresso or strong coffee (cooled)
    - 1/2 cup coffee liqueur (such as Marsala or Kahlua, optional)
- **For Assembly:**
    - 24-30 ladyfingers (savoiardi)
    - Unsweetened cocoa powder (for dusting)
    - Dark chocolate shavings or grated chocolate (optional, for garnish)

**Instructions:**

1. **Prepare Mascarpone Mixture:**
    - In a large bowl, whisk egg yolks and sugar together until pale and slightly thickened.
    - Set the bowl over a pot of simmering water (double boiler) and cook, whisking constantly, for about 8-10 minutes until the mixture is slightly thickened and the sugar is dissolved. Remove from heat and let cool slightly.
    - In a separate bowl, whip the heavy cream until stiff peaks form.
    - Gently fold the mascarpone cheese and vanilla extract into the egg yolk mixture until smooth.
    - Fold the whipped cream into the mascarpone mixture until fully combined.
2. **Prepare Coffee Mixture:**
    - In a shallow dish, combine the cooled espresso or coffee with the coffee liqueur, if using.
3. **Assemble Tiramisu:**
    - Briefly dip each ladyfinger into the coffee mixture, making sure not to soak them. Arrange a layer of dipped ladyfingers in the bottom of a 9x13-inch dish or individual serving glasses.
    - Spread half of the mascarpone mixture over the ladyfingers.
    - Add another layer of dipped ladyfingers on top of the mascarpone mixture.
    - Spread the remaining mascarpone mixture over the second layer of ladyfingers.
4. **Chill:**
    - Cover and refrigerate the tiramisu for at least 4 hours, or overnight, to allow the flavors to meld and the dessert to set.

5. **Serve:**
    - Before serving, dust the top with unsweetened cocoa powder and garnish with dark chocolate shavings or grated chocolate if desired.

Enjoy your rich and creamy Tiramisu!

**Pecan Pie**

**Ingredients:**

- **For the Crust:**
    - 1 1/4 cups all-purpose flour
    - 1/4 teaspoon salt
    - 1/2 cup unsalted butter (cold, cut into cubes)
    - 1/4 cup granulated sugar
    - 1/4 cup ice water
- **For the Filling:**
    - 1 cup light corn syrup
    - 1 cup granulated sugar
    - 1/2 cup unsalted butter (melted)
    - 4 large eggs
    - 1 teaspoon vanilla extract
    - 1/4 teaspoon salt
    - 1 1/2 cups pecan halves

**Instructions:**

1. **Prepare Crust:**
    - In a food processor, combine flour and salt. Add butter and pulse until the mixture resembles coarse crumbs.
    - Gradually add ice water, pulsing until the dough begins to come together.
    - Transfer the dough to a lightly floured surface, shape into a disk, and wrap in plastic. Refrigerate for at least 1 hour.
2. **Preheat Oven:** Preheat your oven to 375°F (190°C).
3. **Roll Out Dough:**
    - On a floured surface, roll out the dough to fit a 9-inch pie pan. Transfer the dough to the pan, trim the edges, and crimp as desired.
4. **Prepare Filling:**
    - In a large bowl, whisk together corn syrup, sugar, melted butter, eggs, vanilla extract, and salt until smooth.
    - Stir in pecan halves.
5. **Fill Pie:** Pour the filling into the prepared pie crust.
6. **Bake:** Bake for 50-60 minutes, or until the filling is set and the crust is golden brown. If the edges of the crust brown too quickly, cover them with foil.
7. **Cool:** Allow the pie to cool completely before slicing.

Enjoy your rich and nutty Pecan Pie!

# Gingerbread Cookies

**Ingredients:**

- **For the Cookies:**
    - 3 1/4 cups all-purpose flour
    - 1/2 teaspoon baking soda
    - 1 tablespoon ground ginger
    - 1 tablespoon ground cinnamon
    - 1/2 teaspoon ground cloves
    - 1/4 teaspoon salt
    - 1/2 cup unsalted butter (room temperature)
    - 1/2 cup granulated sugar
    - 1/2 cup packed brown sugar
    - 1 large egg
    - 1/2 cup unsulfured molasses
- **For the Royal Icing (optional):**
    - 2 large egg whites
    - 3 1/2 cups powdered sugar
    - 1/2 teaspoon lemon juice

**Instructions:**

1. **Preheat Oven:** Preheat your oven to 350°F (175°C). Line baking sheets with parchment paper.
2. **Mix Dry Ingredients:** In a medium bowl, whisk together flour, baking soda, ginger, cinnamon, cloves, and salt.
3. **Cream Butter and Sugars:** In a large bowl, beat the butter, granulated sugar, and brown sugar until light and fluffy.
4. **Add Wet Ingredients:** Beat in the egg and molasses until combined.
5. **Combine Mixtures:** Gradually add the dry ingredients to the wet ingredients, mixing until just combined. The dough will be thick.
6. **Roll Out Dough:** On a floured surface, roll out the dough to 1/4-inch thickness. Cut into shapes with cookie cutters and place on prepared baking sheets.
7. **Bake:** Bake for 8-10 minutes, or until the edges are firm. Allow to cool on the baking sheets for 5 minutes before transferring to a wire rack to cool completely.
8. **Decorate (Optional):** For the royal icing, beat egg whites until foamy. Gradually add powdered sugar and lemon juice, and beat until stiff peaks form. Decorate cooled cookies as desired.

Enjoy your festive and spicy Gingerbread Cookies!

**Vanilla Bean Panna Cotta**

**Ingredients:**

- 2 cups heavy cream
- 1 cup whole milk
- 1/2 cup granulated sugar
- 1 vanilla bean (split and scraped, or 2 teaspoons vanilla extract)
- 1 envelope (2 1/4 teaspoons) unflavored gelatin
- 3 tablespoons cold water

**Instructions:**

1. **Prepare Gelatin:** In a small bowl, sprinkle the gelatin over the cold water and let it bloom for 5 minutes.
2. **Heat Cream Mixture:** In a medium saucepan, combine the cream, milk, and sugar. If using a vanilla bean, add the bean and its seeds to the mixture. Heat over medium heat until the sugar dissolves and the mixture is hot, but not boiling. If using vanilla extract, add it after removing the pan from heat.
3. **Dissolve Gelatin:** Remove the vanilla bean if used. Stir the bloomed gelatin into the hot cream mixture until completely dissolved.
4. **Pour and Chill:** Pour the mixture into serving glasses or ramekins. Refrigerate for at least 4 hours, or until set.
5. **Serve:** Garnish with fresh berries, fruit compote, or a drizzle of caramel sauce if desired.

Enjoy your creamy and elegant Vanilla Bean Panna Cotta!

Maple Bacon Donuts

**Ingredients:**

- **For the Donuts:**
    - 2 cups all-purpose flour
    - 1/2 cup granulated sugar
    - 1/4 cup packed brown sugar
    - 1 tablespoon baking powder
    - 1/2 teaspoon salt
    - 1/2 teaspoon ground cinnamon
    - 1/2 teaspoon ground nutmeg
    - 1/2 cup milk
    - 1/4 cup sour cream
    - 2 large eggs
    - 1/4 cup unsalted butter (melted)
    - 1 teaspoon vanilla extract

- **For the Maple Glaze:**
    - 1 1/2 cups powdered sugar
    - 1/4 cup pure maple syrup
    - 1 tablespoon milk (more if needed for consistency)
- **For the Bacon:**
    - 6 slices bacon (cooked until crispy and crumbled)

**Instructions:**

1. **Preheat Oven:** Preheat your oven to 375°F (190°C). Grease a donut pan or spray it with non-stick cooking spray.
2. **Prepare Dry Ingredients:** In a large bowl, whisk together flour, granulated sugar, brown sugar, baking powder, salt, cinnamon, and nutmeg.
3. **Prepare Wet Ingredients:** In another bowl, combine milk, sour cream, eggs, melted butter, and vanilla extract.
4. **Combine Mixtures:** Pour the wet ingredients into the dry ingredients and stir until just combined. Be careful not to overmix.
5. **Fill Donut Pan:** Spoon the batter into the donut pan, filling each cavity about 2/3 full.
6. **Bake:** Bake for 12-15 minutes, or until a toothpick inserted into the center comes out clean. Allow donuts to cool in the pan for 5 minutes before transferring to a wire rack to cool completely.
7. **Prepare Maple Glaze:** In a bowl, whisk together powdered sugar, maple syrup, and milk until smooth. Adjust the milk as needed to achieve your desired consistency.
8. **Glaze Donuts:** Dip the tops of the cooled donuts into the maple glaze, allowing any excess to drip off.
9. **Add Bacon:** Immediately sprinkle crumbled bacon over the glazed donuts before the glaze sets.

Enjoy your decadent Maple Bacon Donuts!

**Key Lime Pie**

**Ingredients:**

- **For the Crust:**
    - 1 1/2 cups graham cracker crumbs
    - 1/4 cup granulated sugar
    - 1/2 cup unsalted butter (melted)
- **For the Filling:**
    - 4 large egg yolks
    - 1 can (14 oz) sweetened condensed milk
    - 1/2 cup freshly squeezed key lime juice (or regular lime juice)
    - 1 tablespoon lime zest (optional)
- **For the Topping:**
    - 1 cup heavy cream
    - 2 tablespoons powdered sugar
    - Lime zest or lime wedges (for garnish)

**Instructions:**

1. **Preheat Oven:** Preheat your oven to 350°F (175°C).
2. **Prepare Crust:**
    - Mix graham cracker crumbs, sugar, and melted butter in a bowl until combined.
    - Press the mixture into the bottom and up the sides of a 9-inch pie pan.
    - Bake for 8-10 minutes until set. Let cool.
3. **Prepare Filling:**
    - Whisk egg yolks in a bowl until pale and slightly thickened.
    - Add sweetened condensed milk and mix until smooth.
    - Stir in lime juice and zest (if using).
4. **Bake Filling:**
    - Pour the filling into the cooled crust.
    - Bake for 15-20 minutes until the filling is set but slightly jiggly in the center.
    - Let cool to room temperature, then refrigerate for at least 3 hours or overnight.
5. **Prepare Topping:**
    - Whip heavy cream and powdered sugar until stiff peaks form.
    - Spread or pipe the whipped cream over the chilled pie.
6. **Garnish and Serve:**
    - Garnish with additional lime zest or lime wedges if desired.

Enjoy your tangy and creamy Key Lime Pie!

**Spaghetti Carbonara**

**Ingredients:**

- 12 oz (340g) spaghetti
- 4 oz (115g) pancetta or guanciale (diced)
- 2 large eggs
- 1 cup (100g) grated Pecorino Romano or Parmesan cheese
- 2 cloves garlic (minced)
- Salt and freshly ground black pepper
- 2 tablespoons olive oil (optional)
- Fresh parsley (chopped, for garnish, optional)

**Instructions:**

1. **Cook Spaghetti:** Boil salted water and cook spaghetti according to package instructions until al dente. Reserve 1 cup of pasta water, then drain.
2. **Cook Pancetta:** In a large skillet, heat olive oil (if using) over medium heat. Add pancetta and cook until crispy, about 5-7 minutes. Remove from heat.
3. **Prepare Sauce:** Whisk eggs and cheese together in a bowl. Season with salt and pepper.
4. **Combine:** Add minced garlic to the skillet with pancetta and cook for 1 minute. Toss in the hot spaghetti and coat with pancetta and garlic.
5. **Finish:** Remove from heat and quickly mix in the egg mixture, adding reserved pasta water gradually to achieve a creamy consistency.
6. **Serve:** Garnish with chopped parsley and additional cheese if desired.

Enjoy your creamy and flavorful Spaghetti Carbonara!

**Beef Stroganoff**

**Ingredients:**

- 1 lb (450g) beef sirloin or tenderloin (sliced into thin strips)
- 2 tablespoons olive oil
- 1 small onion (chopped)
- 2 cloves garlic (minced)
- 8 oz (225g) mushrooms (sliced)
- 1 tablespoon all-purpose flour
- 1 cup beef broth
- 1 cup sour cream
- 1 tablespoon Dijon mustard
- 1 tablespoon Worcestershire sauce
- Salt and freshly ground black pepper
- Fresh parsley (chopped, for garnish)
- Cooked egg noodles or rice (for serving)

**Instructions:**

1. **Cook Beef:** Heat olive oil in a skillet over medium-high heat. Add beef strips and cook until browned. Remove from skillet and set aside.
2. **Sauté Vegetables:** In the same skillet, add onion and cook until softened. Add garlic and mushrooms, and cook until mushrooms are tender.
3. **Make Sauce:** Sprinkle flour over the vegetables and cook for 1 minute. Gradually add beef broth, stirring constantly. Simmer until slightly thickened.
4. **Combine:** Stir in sour cream, Dijon mustard, and Worcestershire sauce. Return beef to the skillet and simmer until heated through. Season with salt and pepper.
5. **Serve:** Serve over cooked egg noodles or rice. Garnish with chopped parsley.

Enjoy your rich and creamy Beef Stroganoff!

**Chicken Parmesan**

**Ingredients:**

- **For the Chicken:**
    - 4 boneless, skinless chicken breasts
    - 1 cup all-purpose flour
    - 2 large eggs
    - 1 cup breadcrumbs (preferably Italian-seasoned)
    - 1/2 cup grated Parmesan cheese
    - Salt and freshly ground black pepper
    - Olive oil (for frying)
- **For the Sauce:**
    - 2 cups marinara sauce
    - 1 teaspoon dried oregano (optional)
    - 1 teaspoon dried basil (optional)
- **For Assembly:**
    - 1 1/2 cups shredded mozzarella cheese
    - Fresh basil or parsley (chopped, for garnish)
    - Cooked spaghetti or another pasta (for serving)

**Instructions:**

1. **Preheat Oven:** Preheat your oven to 375°F (190°C).
2. **Prepare Chicken:**
    - Place each chicken breast between two sheets of plastic wrap or parchment paper. Pound to an even thickness (about 1/2 inch) using a meat mallet or rolling pin.
3. **Bread Chicken:**
    - Set up a breading station: Place flour in one shallow dish, beaten eggs in another, and a mixture of breadcrumbs and grated Parmesan cheese in a third dish.
    - Season the chicken breasts with salt and pepper. Dredge each breast in flour, dip in beaten eggs, then coat with the breadcrumb mixture, pressing gently to adhere.
4. **Fry Chicken:**
    - Heat olive oil in a large skillet over medium heat. Fry the breaded chicken breasts until golden brown and cooked through, about 4-5 minutes per side. Transfer to a paper towel-lined plate to drain.
5. **Assemble and Bake:**
    - Spread a thin layer of marinara sauce in the bottom of a baking dish. Place the fried chicken breasts on top.

- Spoon additional marinara sauce over each chicken breast and sprinkle with shredded mozzarella cheese.
- Bake for 20-25 minutes, or until the cheese is melted and bubbly.
6. **Garnish and Serve:**
    - Garnish with chopped fresh basil or parsley. Serve over cooked spaghetti or another pasta.

Enjoy your delicious Chicken Parmesan!

**Thai Green Curry**

**Ingredients:**

- **For the Curry:**
    - 2 tablespoons vegetable oil
    - 2-3 tablespoons green curry paste (adjust to taste)
    - 1 can (14 oz) coconut milk
    - 1 cup chicken or vegetable broth
    - 1 tablespoon fish sauce (or soy sauce for a vegetarian option)
    - 1 tablespoon palm sugar or brown sugar
    - 1 cup bamboo shoots (canned or fresh, sliced)
    - 1 red bell pepper (sliced)
    - 1 cup sliced mushrooms (e.g., shiitake or button mushrooms)
    - 1 cup sliced Thai eggplants or regular eggplants (cut into chunks)
    - 1 cup sliced chicken breast or tofu (optional)
    - Fresh Thai basil or cilantro (for garnish)
    - Cooked jasmine rice (for serving)
    - Lime wedges (for garnish)

**Instructions:**

1. **Heat Oil and Curry Paste:**
    - In a large skillet or wok, heat the vegetable oil over medium heat. Add the green curry paste and cook for 1-2 minutes until fragrant.
2. **Add Liquids:**
    - Pour in the coconut milk and chicken or vegetable broth. Stir well to combine with the curry paste. Bring to a simmer.
3. **Flavor the Curry:**
    - Stir in the fish sauce (or soy sauce) and sugar. Adjust the seasoning to taste.
4. **Cook Vegetables:**
    - Add the bamboo shoots, bell pepper, mushrooms, and eggplants to the skillet. Simmer for about 5-7 minutes, until the vegetables are tender.
5. **Add Protein:**
    - If using chicken or tofu, add it to the curry. Cook until the chicken is cooked through or the tofu is heated.
6. **Simmer and Adjust:**
    - Continue to simmer for another 5-10 minutes, allowing the flavors to meld together. Adjust seasoning if necessary.
7. **Serve:**
    - Serve the curry hot over cooked jasmine rice. Garnish with fresh Thai basil or cilantro and lime wedges.

Enjoy your aromatic and spicy Thai Green Curry!

## Shrimp Scampi

### Ingredients:

- 1 lb (450g) large shrimp (peeled and deveined)
- 8 oz (225g) linguine or spaghetti
- 3 tablespoons unsalted butter
- 2 tablespoons olive oil
- 4 cloves garlic (minced)
- 1/2 cup dry white wine (or chicken broth)
- Juice of 1 lemon
- 1/4 teaspoon red pepper flakes (optional)
- Salt and freshly ground black pepper
- 1/4 cup chopped fresh parsley
- Lemon wedges (for serving)

### Instructions:

1. **Cook Pasta:**
    - Cook linguine or spaghetti according to package instructions until al dente. Reserve 1/2 cup of pasta water, then drain and set aside.
2. **Prepare Shrimp:**
    - Season the shrimp with salt and pepper.
3. **Sauté Garlic:**
    - In a large skillet, heat butter and olive oil over medium heat. Add minced garlic and cook for about 1 minute until fragrant, but not browned.
4. **Cook Shrimp:**
    - Add the shrimp to the skillet and cook for 2-3 minutes per side until pink and opaque. Remove the shrimp from the skillet and set aside.
5. **Make Sauce:**
    - Pour the white wine (or chicken broth) and lemon juice into the skillet, scraping up any browned bits from the bottom of the pan. Bring to a simmer and cook for 2-3 minutes until slightly reduced.
6. **Combine Pasta and Shrimp:**
    - Return the shrimp to the skillet. Add the cooked pasta and toss to coat in the sauce. If the sauce is too thick, add a bit of reserved pasta water.
7. **Finish and Serve:**
    - Stir in red pepper flakes (if using) and chopped parsley. Adjust seasoning with salt and pepper as needed.
    - Serve immediately with lemon wedges.

Enjoy your flavorful Shrimp Scampi!

**Veggie Stir-Fry**

**Ingredients:**

- 2 tablespoons vegetable oil
- 1 bell pepper (sliced)
- 1 cup broccoli florets
- 1 cup snap peas or sugar snap peas
- 1 carrot (sliced thinly)
- 1 cup mushrooms (sliced)
- 2 cloves garlic (minced)
- 1 tablespoon fresh ginger (grated)
- 1/4 cup soy sauce or tamari
- 2 tablespoons hoisin sauce
- 1 tablespoon rice vinegar
- 1 teaspoon sesame oil
- 1 tablespoon cornstarch (optional, mixed with 2 tablespoons water for thickening)
- Cooked rice or noodles (for serving)
- Sesame seeds and sliced green onions (for garnish)

**Instructions:**

1. **Prepare Ingredients:**
    - Slice vegetables and mix the cornstarch with water if using for thickening.
2. **Heat Oil:**
    - Heat vegetable oil in a large skillet or wok over medium-high heat.
3. **Stir-Fry Vegetables:**
    - Add bell pepper, broccoli, snap peas, carrot, and mushrooms to the skillet. Stir-fry for 3-4 minutes until vegetables are tender-crisp.
4. **Add Aromatics:**
    - Add garlic and ginger, cooking for 1 minute until fragrant.
5. **Add Sauce:**
    - Stir in soy sauce, hoisin sauce, rice vinegar, and sesame oil. Cook for another 1-2 minutes until heated through. If using, add the cornstarch mixture and stir until the sauce thickens.
6. **Serve:**
    - Serve the stir-fry over cooked rice or noodles. Garnish with sesame seeds and sliced green onions.

Enjoy your vibrant and flavorful Veggie Stir-Fry!

**Classic Meatloaf**

**Ingredients:**

**For the Meatloaf:**

1 lb (450g) ground beef

1/2 lb (225g) ground pork

1 small onion (chopped)

2 cloves garlic (minced)

1 cup breadcrumbs

1/2 cup milk

1 large egg

1 tablespoon Worcestershire sauce

1 teaspoon dried thyme

1 teaspoon dried oregano

Salt and freshly ground black pepper

**For the Glaze:**

1/4 cup ketchup

2 tablespoons brown sugar

1 tablespoon Dijon mustard

Instructions:

**Preheat Oven:**

Preheat your oven to 350°F (175°C).

Prepare Meat Mixture:

In a large bowl, combine ground beef, ground pork, chopped onion, minced garlic, breadcrumbs, milk, egg, Worcestershire sauce, thyme, oregano, salt, and pepper. Mix until just combined; do not overmix.

**Shape and Bake:**

Transfer the mixture to a loaf pan and shape it into a loaf. Smooth the top with a spatula.

Prepare Glaze:

In a small bowl, mix ketchup, brown sugar, and Dijon mustard. Spread the mixture evenly over the top of the meatloaf.

**Bake:**

Bake in the preheated oven for 1 hour, or until the internal temperature reaches 160°F (70°C) and the meatloaf is cooked through.

Rest and Serve:

Let the meatloaf rest for 10 minutes before slicing. Serve with your favorite sides.

Enjoy your hearty and comforting Classic Meatloaf!

**Creamy Tomato Basil Soup**

**Ingredients:**

- 2 tablespoons olive oil
- 1 medium onion (chopped)
- 2 cloves garlic (minced)
- 2 cans (14.5 oz each) diced tomatoes
- 2 cups chicken or vegetable broth
- 1/2 cup heavy cream
- 1/4 cup fresh basil leaves (chopped)
- 1 teaspoon sugar (optional)
- Salt and freshly ground black pepper (to taste)
- Fresh basil leaves (for garnish, optional)

**Instructions:**

1. **Sauté Vegetables:**
    - Heat olive oil in a large pot over medium heat. Add chopped onion and cook until softened, about 5 minutes. Add garlic and cook for another 1 minute.
2. **Add Tomatoes and Broth:**
    - Stir in the diced tomatoes and broth. Bring to a simmer and cook for 15-20 minutes to blend flavors.
3. **Blend Soup:**
    - Use an immersion blender to puree the soup until smooth. Alternatively, carefully transfer the soup in batches to a blender and blend until smooth.
4. **Add Cream and Basil:**
    - Return the soup to the pot (if using a blender). Stir in the heavy cream and chopped basil. Cook over low heat for 5 minutes, adding sugar if desired to balance acidity. Season with salt and pepper to taste.
5. **Serve:**
    - Ladle the soup into bowls and garnish with fresh basil leaves if desired.

Enjoy your creamy and flavorful Tomato Basil Soup!

**BBQ Ribs**

**Ingredients:**

- 2 racks baby back ribs (about 2 lbs each)
- 1/4 cup brown sugar
- 2 tablespoons paprika
- 1 tablespoon garlic powder
- 1 tablespoon onion powder
- 1 tablespoon chili powder
- 1 teaspoon ground cumin
- 1 teaspoon salt
- 1/2 teaspoon black pepper
- 1 cup BBQ sauce (your favorite brand)

**Instructions:**

1. **Preheat Oven:** Preheat your oven to 300°F (150°C).
2. **Prepare Ribs:**
   - Remove the membrane from the back of the ribs if not already done.
   - In a small bowl, mix brown sugar, paprika, garlic powder, onion powder, chili powder, cumin, salt, and pepper.
3. **Season Ribs:**
   - Rub the spice mixture all over the ribs, coating them evenly.
4. **Wrap and Bake:**
   - Place each rack of ribs on a large piece of aluminum foil and wrap tightly. Place the wrapped ribs on a baking sheet.
   - Bake in the preheated oven for 2.5 to 3 hours, until the ribs are tender.
5. **Add BBQ Sauce:**
   - Preheat your grill to medium-high heat. Remove the ribs from the foil and discard any accumulated juices.
   - Brush the ribs with BBQ sauce and grill for 5-10 minutes, turning occasionally and basting with more sauce, until caramelized and slightly crispy.
6. **Serve:**
   - Let the ribs rest for a few minutes before cutting into individual portions. Serve with additional BBQ sauce on the side.

Enjoy your flavorful and tender BBQ Ribs!

**Chicken and Waffles**

**Ingredients:**

**For the Fried Chicken:**

4 boneless, skinless chicken breasts or thighs

1 cup buttermilk

1 cup all-purpose flour

1 teaspoon paprika

1 teaspoon garlic powder

1 teaspoon onion powder

1/2 teaspoon salt

1/2 teaspoon black pepper

Vegetable oil (for frying)

**For the Waffles:**

2 cups all-purpose flour

2 tablespoons sugar

1 tablespoon baking powder

1/2 teaspoon salt

2 large eggs

1 3/4 cups milk

1/2 cup unsalted butter (melted)

1 teaspoon vanilla extract

**For Serving:**

Maple syrup

Butter (optional)

Powdered sugar (optional)

Instructions:

**Prepare Chicken:**

Soak the chicken in buttermilk for at least 1 hour or overnight in the refrigerator.

Prepare Flour Coating:

In a bowl, mix flour, paprika, garlic powder, onion powder, salt, and pepper.

**Coat Chicken:**

Remove chicken from buttermilk, letting excess drip off. Dredge each piece in the seasoned flour, pressing gently to coat evenly.

**Fry Chicken:**

Heat vegetable oil in a large skillet or Dutch oven over medium-high heat to about 350°F (175°C).

Fry chicken in batches, cooking for about 6-8 minutes per side, until golden brown and cooked through. Transfer to a paper towel-lined plate to drain.

**Prepare Waffles:**

Preheat your waffle iron according to the manufacturer's instructions.

In a large bowl, whisk together flour, sugar, baking powder, and salt.

In another bowl, beat eggs, then mix in milk, melted butter, and vanilla extract. Combine wet and dry ingredients, stirring until just mixed (batter may be lumpy).

Pour batter into the preheated waffle iron and cook according to the manufacturer's instructions until waffles are golden brown.

**Serve:**

Serve the fried chicken on top of the waffles. Drizzle with maple syrup and add a pat of butter if desired. Sprinkle with powdered sugar for a touch of sweetness.

Enjoy your hearty and delicious Chicken and Waffles!

**Baked Ziti**

**Ingredients:**

- 1 lb (450g) ziti pasta
- 2 tablespoons olive oil
- 1 lb (450g) Italian sausage (casings removed, crumbled)
- 1 onion (chopped)
- 2 cloves garlic (minced)
- 1 can (28 oz) crushed tomatoes
- 1 can (15 oz) tomato sauce
- 1/4 cup tomato paste
- 1 teaspoon dried basil
- 1 teaspoon dried oregano
- 1/2 teaspoon red pepper flakes (optional)
- Salt and freshly ground black pepper (to taste)
- 2 cups ricotta cheese
- 2 cups shredded mozzarella cheese
- 1/2 cup grated Parmesan cheese
- Fresh basil or parsley (for garnish, optional)

**Instructions:**

1. **Cook Pasta:**
    - Preheat your oven to 375°F (190°C). Cook the ziti pasta according to package instructions until al dente. Drain and set aside.
2. **Prepare Sauce:**
    - In a large skillet, heat olive oil over medium heat. Add crumbled Italian sausage and cook until browned. Remove sausage and set aside.
    - In the same skillet, add chopped onion and cook until softened. Add garlic and cook for 1 minute more.
    - Stir in crushed tomatoes, tomato sauce, tomato paste, dried basil, oregano, red pepper flakes, and salt and pepper. Simmer for 10 minutes.
3. **Combine Ingredients:**
    - Stir the cooked sausage into the sauce.
    - In a large bowl, mix cooked pasta with the ricotta cheese. Stir in a portion of the sauce mixture, reserving some for topping.
4. **Assemble Dish:**
    - In a baking dish, spread a thin layer of the reserved sauce on the bottom. Layer half of the pasta mixture in the dish. Top with a portion of the mozzarella cheese and some of the remaining sauce. Repeat layers with the remaining pasta, sauce, and mozzarella. Sprinkle Parmesan cheese on top.
5. **Bake:**

- Bake in the preheated oven for 25-30 minutes, or until the cheese is melted and bubbly, and the top is golden brown.
6. **Garnish and Serve:**
    - Garnish with fresh basil or parsley if desired. Let cool slightly before serving.

Enjoy your hearty and cheesy Baked Ziti!

**Stuffed Bell Peppers**

**Ingredients:**

- 4 large bell peppers (any color)
- 1 tablespoon olive oil
- 1/2 cup onion (chopped)
- 2 cloves garlic (minced)
- 1/2 lb (225g) ground beef or turkey
- 1 cup cooked rice (white or brown)
- 1 cup tomato sauce (or diced tomatoes)
- 1 teaspoon dried oregano
- 1 teaspoon dried basil
- 1/2 teaspoon paprika
- 1/2 cup shredded cheese (cheddar, mozzarella, or a blend)
- Salt and freshly ground black pepper (to taste)
- Fresh parsley or basil (for garnish, optional)

**Instructions:**

1. **Preheat Oven:**
    - Preheat your oven to 375°F (190°C).
2. **Prepare Peppers:**
    - Cut the tops off the bell peppers and remove the seeds and membranes. If needed, trim the bottoms slightly to ensure they stand upright (be careful not to cut through the pepper).
3. **Cook Filling:**
    - Heat olive oil in a large skillet over medium heat. Add chopped onion and cook until softened, about 5 minutes. Add garlic and cook for an additional minute.
    - Add ground beef or turkey to the skillet. Cook until browned, breaking it up with a spoon. Drain excess fat if necessary.
    - Stir in cooked rice, tomato sauce, oregano, basil, paprika, salt, and pepper. Cook for 5 minutes, allowing the flavors to meld.
4. **Stuff Peppers:**
    - Spoon the filling into each bell pepper, packing it down lightly. Place stuffed peppers in a baking dish.
5. **Bake:**
    - Cover the baking dish with aluminum foil and bake for 30 minutes. Remove the foil and sprinkle shredded cheese on top of each pepper.
    - Continue baking uncovered for an additional 10-15 minutes, or until the peppers are tender and the cheese is melted and bubbly.
6. **Serve:**
    - Garnish with fresh parsley or basil if desired. Serve hot.

Enjoy your flavorful and hearty Stuffed Bell Peppers!

**Fettuccine Alfredo**

**Ingredients:**

- 12 oz (340g) fettuccine pasta
- 1/2 cup (1 stick) unsalted butter
- 1 cup heavy cream
- 1 cup grated Parmesan cheese
- 2 cloves garlic (minced)
- Salt and freshly ground black pepper (to taste)
- Fresh parsley (chopped, for garnish, optional)

**Instructions:**

1. **Cook Pasta:**
    - Cook the fettuccine according to package instructions until al dente. Reserve 1/2 cup of pasta water, then drain and set aside.
2. **Prepare Sauce:**
    - In a large skillet, melt the butter over medium heat. Add minced garlic and cook for about 1 minute until fragrant, but not browned.
3. **Add Cream:**
    - Pour in the heavy cream and simmer for 2-3 minutes, stirring occasionally, until it starts to thicken.
4. **Finish Sauce:**
    - Stir in the grated Parmesan cheese until melted and smooth. Season with salt and black pepper to taste.
5. **Combine Pasta and Sauce:**
    - Add the cooked fettuccine to the skillet with the Alfredo sauce. Toss to coat the pasta, adding a bit of reserved pasta water if needed to achieve the desired consistency.
6. **Serve:**
    - Garnish with chopped parsley if desired and serve immediately.

Enjoy your creamy and delicious Fettuccine Alfredo!

**Beef Tacos**

**Ingredients:**

- **For the Beef Filling:**
    - 1 lb (450g) ground beef
    - 1 tablespoon olive oil
    - 1 small onion (chopped)
    - 2 cloves garlic (minced)
    - 1 packet (1 oz) taco seasoning mix (or homemade, see below)
    - 1/2 cup water
    - Salt and freshly ground black pepper (to taste)
- **For the Taco Seasoning (optional, if not using a packet):**
    - 1 tablespoon chili powder
    - 1 teaspoon ground cumin
    - 1 teaspoon paprika
    - 1/2 teaspoon garlic powder
    - 1/2 teaspoon onion powder
    - 1/4 teaspoon cayenne pepper (optional)
    - 1/4 teaspoon dried oregano
    - 1/4 teaspoon salt
    - 1/4 teaspoon black pepper
- **For Serving:**
    - Taco shells or tortillas
    - Shredded lettuce
    - Diced tomatoes
    - Shredded cheese (cheddar, Monterey Jack, or your choice)
    - Sour cream
    - Salsa
    - Sliced jalapeños (optional)
    - Chopped fresh cilantro (optional)

**Instructions:**

1. **Cook Beef:**
    - Heat olive oil in a large skillet over medium-high heat. Add chopped onion and cook until softened, about 5 minutes. Add minced garlic and cook for another 1 minute.
2. **Brown Beef:**
    - Add ground beef to the skillet. Cook, breaking it up with a spoon, until browned and cooked through. Drain excess fat if necessary.
3. **Season Beef:**

- Stir in taco seasoning mix or homemade seasoning. Add 1/2 cup water and simmer for 5 minutes, allowing the flavors to meld and the sauce to thicken. Season with salt and pepper to taste.
4. **Prepare Taco Shells:**
    - While the beef is simmering, heat taco shells or tortillas according to package instructions.
5. **Assemble Tacos:**
    - Spoon the seasoned beef into taco shells or tortillas. Top with shredded lettuce, diced tomatoes, shredded cheese, and any other desired toppings such as sour cream, salsa, sliced jalapeños, or chopped cilantro.
6. **Serve:**
    - Serve immediately and enjoy!

These Beef Tacos are flavorful and perfect for a quick meal or a casual gathering.

**Moroccan Tagine**

**Ingredients:**

- **For the Tagine:**
    - 2 lbs (900g) chicken thighs or lamb (cut into chunks)
    - 2 tablespoons olive oil
    - 1 large onion (chopped)
    - 3 cloves garlic (minced)
    - 1 teaspoon ground cumin
    - 1 teaspoon ground coriander
    - 1 teaspoon ground turmeric
    - 1 teaspoon ground ginger
    - 1/2 teaspoon ground cinnamon
    - 1/4 teaspoon ground cayenne pepper (optional, for heat)
    - 1 can (14.5 oz) diced tomatoes
    - 1 cup chicken or vegetable broth
    - 1/2 cup dried apricots (chopped)
    - 1/2 cup green olives (pitted and sliced)
    - 1/2 cup almonds (toasted)
    - 1/4 cup honey
    - 1 cup cooked chickpeas (optional)
    - Salt and freshly ground black pepper (to taste)
    - Fresh cilantro or parsley (for garnish)
- **For Serving:**
    - Couscous or rice

**Instructions:**

1. **Prepare Ingredients:**
    - If using chicken, pat the pieces dry with paper towels. Season with salt and pepper.
2. **Sear Meat:**
    - Heat olive oil in a large tagine or Dutch oven over medium-high heat. Add the meat and brown on all sides. Remove from the pot and set aside.
3. **Cook Aromatics:**
    - In the same pot, add chopped onion and cook until softened, about 5 minutes. Add minced garlic and cook for 1 minute more.
4. **Add Spices:**
    - Stir in cumin, coriander, turmeric, ginger, cinnamon, and cayenne pepper (if using). Cook for 1 minute until fragrant.
5. **Simmer Tagine:**

- Return the browned meat to the pot. Stir in diced tomatoes and broth. Bring to a simmer.
- Cover and reduce heat to low. Cook for 1.5 to 2 hours, or until the meat is tender and cooked through.

6. **Add Dried Fruit and Nuts:**
    - Stir in dried apricots and honey. If using chickpeas, add them now. Simmer for another 10-15 minutes until the sauce is thickened.
7. **Garnish and Serve:**
    - Stir in sliced green olives and toasted almonds just before serving.
    - Garnish with chopped fresh cilantro or parsley.
    - Serve over couscous or rice.

Enjoy your aromatic and flavorful Moroccan Tagine!

**Chicken Pot Pie**

**Ingredients:**

- **For the Filling:**
    - 2 tablespoons butter
    - 1 medium onion (chopped)
    - 2 cloves garlic (minced)
    - 1 cup carrots (diced)
    - 1 cup celery (diced)
    - 1 cup frozen peas
    - 2 cups cooked chicken (shredded or cubed)
    - 1/4 cup all-purpose flour
    - 1 1/2 cups chicken broth
    - 1/2 cup milk or heavy cream
    - 1 teaspoon dried thyme
    - 1/2 teaspoon dried rosemary
    - Salt and freshly ground black pepper (to taste)
- **For the Crust:**
    - 1 package (14.1 oz) refrigerated pie crusts (or homemade crust)
    - 1 egg (beaten, for egg wash)

**Instructions:**

1. **Preheat Oven:**
    - Preheat your oven to 425°F (220°C).
2. **Prepare Filling:**
    - In a large skillet, melt butter over medium heat. Add onion, garlic, carrots, and celery. Cook until vegetables are softened, about 5-7 minutes.
    - Stir in flour and cook for 1-2 minutes to form a roux. Gradually add chicken broth and milk, stirring constantly, until the mixture thickens.
    - Add cooked chicken, peas, thyme, rosemary, salt, and pepper. Mix well and cook for another 2-3 minutes. Remove from heat.
3. **Assemble Pie:**
    - Roll out one pie crust and fit it into a 9-inch pie dish. Trim excess crust hanging over the edges.
    - Pour the chicken mixture into the pie crust.
    - Roll out the second pie crust and place it over the filling. Trim excess crust and pinch the edges to seal. Cut a few slits in the top crust to allow steam to escape.
    - Brush the top with beaten egg.
4. **Bake:**
    - Place the pie on a baking sheet to catch any drips. Bake for 30-35 minutes, or until the crust is golden brown and the filling is bubbling.

5. **Cool and Serve:**
    - Let the pie cool for 10 minutes before slicing. Serve warm.

Enjoy your comforting and delicious Chicken Pot Pie!

**Stuffed Mushrooms**

**Ingredients:**

- 12 large button mushrooms (stems removed and finely chopped)
- 2 tablespoons olive oil
- 1 small onion (chopped)
- 2 cloves garlic (minced)
- 1/2 cup breadcrumbs (plain or seasoned)
- 1/4 cup grated Parmesan cheese
- 1/4 cup cream cheese (softened)
- 1/4 cup chopped fresh parsley (or basil)
- Salt and freshly ground black pepper (to taste)
- Additional Parmesan cheese for topping (optional)

**Instructions:**

1. **Preheat Oven:**
    - Preheat your oven to 375°F (190°C).
2. **Prepare Mushroom Caps:**
    - Clean the mushroom caps with a damp paper towel. Arrange them on a baking sheet or in a baking dish.
3. **Cook Filling:**
    - Heat olive oil in a skillet over medium heat. Add chopped mushroom stems, onion, and garlic. Sauté until the mixture is tender and most of the moisture has evaporated, about 5 minutes.
4. **Combine Ingredients:**
    - In a bowl, mix the cooked mushroom stem mixture with breadcrumbs, Parmesan cheese, cream cheese, and parsley. Season with salt and pepper.
5. **Stuff Mushrooms:**
    - Spoon the filling into the mushroom caps, pressing down slightly to pack it in. Sprinkle additional Parmesan cheese on top if desired.
6. **Bake:**
    - Bake the stuffed mushrooms in the preheated oven for 20-25 minutes, or until the tops are golden brown and the mushrooms are tender.
7. **Serve:**
    - Garnish with extra parsley if desired and serve warm.

Enjoy your flavorful and savory Stuffed Mushrooms!

**Eggplant Parmesan**

**Ingredients:**

- 2 large eggplants (sliced into 1/4-inch rounds)
- 1/4 cup olive oil (for brushing)
- 1 cup all-purpose flour
- 3 large eggs (beaten)
- 2 cups breadcrumbs (plain or seasoned)
- 2 cups marinara sauce
- 2 cups shredded mozzarella cheese
- 1/2 cup grated Parmesan cheese
- 1/4 cup fresh basil leaves (chopped, or dried basil)
- Salt and freshly ground black pepper (to taste)

**Instructions:**

1. **Prepare Eggplant:**
   - Preheat your oven to 400°F (200°C).
   - Place eggplant slices on a baking sheet. Brush both sides with olive oil and sprinkle with salt. Bake for 20 minutes, flipping halfway through, until slices are tender and slightly golden. Remove from oven and set aside.
2. **Bread Eggplant:**
   - Set up a breading station with three shallow dishes: flour in one, beaten eggs in the second, and breadcrumbs in the third.
   - Dredge each eggplant slice in flour, then dip in beaten eggs, and coat with breadcrumbs.
3. **Fry Eggplant:**
   - Heat a few tablespoons of olive oil in a large skillet over medium heat. Fry the breaded eggplant slices in batches until golden brown on both sides, about 2-3 minutes per side. Drain on paper towels.
4. **Assemble Dish:**
   - In a baking dish, spread a thin layer of marinara sauce on the bottom. Arrange a layer of eggplant slices over the sauce.
   - Spoon more marinara sauce over the eggplant, then sprinkle with mozzarella cheese and Parmesan cheese.
   - Repeat layers, finishing with a layer of sauce and cheese on top.
5. **Bake:**
   - Bake in the preheated oven for 25-30 minutes, or until the cheese is bubbly and golden brown.
6. **Garnish and Serve:**
   - Garnish with fresh basil before serving. Let the dish cool for a few minutes before slicing.

Enjoy your delicious and cheesy Eggplant Parmesan!

**Fish Tacos**

**Ingredients:**

- **For the Fish:**
    - 1 lb (450g) white fish fillets (such as cod, tilapia, or mahi-mahi)
    - 1/2 cup all-purpose flour
    - 1/2 cup cornmeal
    - 1 teaspoon paprika
    - 1 teaspoon ground cumin
    - 1/2 teaspoon garlic powder
    - 1/2 teaspoon onion powder
    - 1/2 teaspoon salt
    - 1/4 teaspoon black pepper
    - 1/2 cup buttermilk
    - Vegetable oil (for frying)
- **For the Slaw:**
    - 2 cups shredded cabbage (green or red)
    - 1/2 cup shredded carrots
    - 1/4 cup chopped fresh cilantro
    - 1/4 cup mayonnaise
    - 2 tablespoons lime juice
    - 1 tablespoon honey
    - Salt and pepper (to taste)
- **For Serving:**
    - 8 small corn or flour tortillas
    - 1 avocado (sliced)
    - Lime wedges (for garnish)
    - Salsa or pico de gallo (optional)

**Instructions:**

1. **Prepare the Fish:**
    - Cut the fish fillets into strips or bite-sized pieces.
    - In a shallow bowl, mix flour, cornmeal, paprika, cumin, garlic powder, onion powder, salt, and pepper.
    - Dip each piece of fish into buttermilk, then dredge in the flour mixture, coating evenly.
2. **Fry the Fish:**
    - Heat vegetable oil in a large skillet over medium-high heat (about 1/2 inch of oil).
    - Fry the coated fish pieces in batches until golden brown and cooked through, about 3-4 minutes per side. Transfer to a paper towel-lined plate to drain.
3. **Prepare the Slaw:**

- In a large bowl, combine shredded cabbage, shredded carrots, and chopped cilantro.
- In a small bowl, whisk together mayonnaise, lime juice, honey, salt, and pepper. Pour over the cabbage mixture and toss to coat.

4. **Warm Tortillas:**
   - Warm the tortillas in a dry skillet over medium heat or in the oven wrapped in foil.
5. **Assemble Tacos:**
   - Place a few pieces of fried fish in each tortilla. Top with slaw, avocado slices, and additional salsa or pico de gallo if desired.
   - Garnish with lime wedges.
6. **Serve:**
   - Serve the fish tacos immediately with extra lime wedges on the side.

Enjoy your fresh and flavorful Fish Tacos!

**Pulled Pork Sandwiches**

**Ingredients:**

- **For the Pork:**
    - 3-4 lbs (1.4-1.8 kg) pork shoulder (also known as pork butt)
    - 1 tablespoon olive oil
    - 1 tablespoon paprika
    - 1 tablespoon brown sugar
    - 1 teaspoon garlic powder
    - 1 teaspoon onion powder
    - 1 teaspoon ground cumin
    - 1/2 teaspoon ground black pepper
    - 1/2 teaspoon salt
    - 1 cup BBQ sauce (your favorite brand)
- **For Serving:**
    - 8 hamburger buns
    - Coleslaw (optional, for topping)
    - Pickles (optional)

**Instructions:**

1. **Prepare the Pork:**
    - In a small bowl, mix paprika, brown sugar, garlic powder, onion powder, cumin, pepper, and salt.
    - Rub the spice mixture all over the pork shoulder.
2. **Cook the Pork:**
    - Heat olive oil in a large skillet over medium-high heat. Sear the pork shoulder on all sides until browned, about 3-4 minutes per side. Transfer to a slow cooker.
    - Pour 1/2 cup of BBQ sauce over the pork. Cover and cook on low for 8-10 hours, or on high for 4-6 hours, until the pork is tender and easily shreddable.
3. **Shred the Pork:**
    - Remove the pork from the slow cooker and shred it using two forks. Return the shredded pork to the slow cooker and mix with the remaining BBQ sauce. Let it cook on low for an additional 30 minutes to absorb the flavors.
4. **Prepare Sandwiches:**
    - Toast the hamburger buns if desired. Pile the pulled pork onto the bottom half of each bun.
5. **Serve:**
    - Top with coleslaw and pickles if using. Cover with the top half of the bun and serve.

Enjoy your savory and satisfying Pulled Pork Sandwiches!

**Garlic Herb Mashed Potatoes**

**Ingredients:**

- 2 lbs (900g) potatoes (russet or Yukon Gold), peeled and cut into chunks
- 4 cloves garlic, peeled
- 1/2 cup (1 stick) unsalted butter
- 1/2 cup milk (whole or 2%)
- 1/4 cup heavy cream (optional, for extra creaminess)
- 1/4 cup chopped fresh herbs (such as parsley, chives, or thyme)
- Salt and freshly ground black pepper (to taste)

**Instructions:**

1. **Cook Potatoes:**
    - Place the potatoes and garlic cloves in a large pot. Cover with cold water and add a pinch of salt.
    - Bring to a boil over high heat. Reduce heat to medium and cook until potatoes are tender and easily pierced with a fork, about 15-20 minutes.
2. **Drain and Mash:**
    - Drain the potatoes and garlic thoroughly and return them to the pot.
    - Add butter to the hot potatoes and garlic. Mash until smooth and creamy, using a potato masher or ricer.
3. **Add Dairy:**
    - Warm the milk and heavy cream in a small saucepan or microwave. Gradually add the warm milk and cream to the mashed potatoes, stirring until the desired consistency is reached. You can adjust the amount of liquid based on how creamy you like your potatoes.
4. **Season and Herb:**
    - Stir in the chopped fresh herbs. Season with salt and pepper to taste.
5. **Serve:**
    - Transfer the mashed potatoes to a serving dish and garnish with additional herbs or a pat of butter if desired.

Enjoy your flavorful Garlic Herb Mashed Potatoes!

**Sweet Potato Fries**

**Ingredients:**

- 2 large sweet potatoes (peeled and cut into thin fries)
- 2 tablespoons olive oil
- 1 teaspoon paprika
- 1/2 teaspoon garlic powder
- 1/2 teaspoon onion powder
- 1/2 teaspoon ground cumin
- 1/4 teaspoon cayenne pepper (optional, for heat)
- Salt and freshly ground black pepper (to taste)

**Instructions:**

1. **Preheat Oven:**
   - Preheat your oven to 425°F (220°C). Line a baking sheet with parchment paper or lightly grease it.
2. **Prepare Sweet Potatoes:**
   - Place the cut sweet potatoes in a large bowl. Toss with olive oil, ensuring they are evenly coated.
3. **Season Fries:**
   - In a small bowl, mix paprika, garlic powder, onion powder, cumin, cayenne pepper (if using), salt, and pepper. Sprinkle the seasoning mix over the sweet potatoes and toss to coat evenly.
4. **Bake:**
   - Spread the sweet potatoes in a single layer on the prepared baking sheet, avoiding overcrowding for crispier fries.
   - Bake for 20-25 minutes, flipping halfway through, until the fries are golden and crispy.
5. **Serve:**
   - Let cool slightly before serving. Enjoy with your favorite dipping sauce.

Enjoy your crispy and flavorful Sweet Potato Fries!

## Cauliflower Rice

**Ingredients:**

- 1 large head of cauliflower
- 1-2 tablespoons olive oil (or butter)
- 1 small onion (chopped, optional)
- 2 cloves garlic (minced, optional)
- Salt and freshly ground black pepper (to taste)
- Fresh herbs (such as parsley or cilantro, for garnish, optional)

**Instructions:**

1. **Prepare Cauliflower:**
   - Remove the leaves and stem from the cauliflower head. Cut it into florets.
2. **Rice the Cauliflower:**
   - In a food processor, pulse the cauliflower florets in batches until they resemble the size and texture of rice grains. Be careful not to over-process; you want a rice-like texture, not mushy cauliflower.
3. **Cook Cauliflower Rice:**
   - Heat olive oil (or butter) in a large skillet over medium heat. If using onion and garlic, add them to the skillet and cook until softened and fragrant, about 3-5 minutes.
   - Add the riced cauliflower to the skillet. Cook, stirring occasionally, for about 5-7 minutes, until the cauliflower is tender and has reached your desired texture. Season with salt and pepper to taste.
4. **Serve:**
   - Garnish with fresh herbs if desired. Serve as a side dish or base for your favorite main course.

Enjoy your versatile and healthy Cauliflower Rice!

## Crispy Brussels Sprouts

**Ingredients:**

- 1 lb (450g) Brussels sprouts
- 2 tablespoons olive oil
- 1 teaspoon garlic powder
- 1 teaspoon onion powder
- 1/2 teaspoon smoked paprika (or regular paprika)
- 1/4 teaspoon salt
- 1/4 teaspoon freshly ground black pepper
- 2 tablespoons grated Parmesan cheese (optional, for added flavor)
- Lemon wedges (for serving, optional)

**Instructions:**

1. **Preheat Oven:**
    - Preheat your oven to 425°F (220°C). Line a baking sheet with parchment paper or lightly grease it.
2. **Prepare Brussels Sprouts:**
    - Trim the ends of the Brussels sprouts and remove any outer leaves that are damaged. Cut the sprouts in half lengthwise.
3. **Season:**
    - In a large bowl, toss the Brussels sprouts with olive oil, garlic powder, onion powder, paprika, salt, and pepper. Make sure the sprouts are evenly coated.
4. **Roast:**
    - Spread the Brussels sprouts in a single layer on the prepared baking sheet. Avoid overcrowding to ensure they get crispy.
    - Roast in the preheated oven for 20-25 minutes, or until the sprouts are crispy and caramelized, stirring halfway through the cooking time for even roasting.
5. **Finish and Serve:**
    - If using Parmesan cheese, sprinkle it over the Brussels sprouts during the last 5 minutes of roasting.
    - Serve warm with lemon wedges on the side if desired.

Enjoy your crispy, delicious Brussels sprouts!

## Quinoa Salad

**Ingredients:**

- 1 cup quinoa
- 2 cups water or vegetable broth (for cooking quinoa)
- 1 cup cherry tomatoes (halved)
- 1 cucumber (diced)
- 1/2 red onion (finely chopped)
- 1/4 cup Kalamata olives (pitted and sliced)
- 1/4 cup feta cheese (crumbled, optional)
- 1/4 cup fresh parsley (chopped)
- 2 tablespoons extra-virgin olive oil
- 1 tablespoon lemon juice
- 1 teaspoon Dijon mustard
- 1 garlic clove (minced)
- Salt and freshly ground black pepper (to taste)

**Instructions:**

1. **Cook Quinoa:**
   - Rinse the quinoa under cold water. In a medium saucepan, bring 2 cups of water or vegetable broth to a boil.
   - Add the quinoa, reduce heat to low, cover, and simmer for about 15 minutes, or until the quinoa is cooked and the liquid is absorbed. Fluff with a fork and let it cool to room temperature.
2. **Prepare Vegetables:**
   - While the quinoa is cooling, prepare the vegetables. In a large bowl, combine cherry tomatoes, cucumber, red onion, olives, and parsley.
3. **Make Dressing:**
   - In a small bowl or jar, whisk together olive oil, lemon juice, Dijon mustard, minced garlic, salt, and pepper.
4. **Assemble Salad:**
   - Once the quinoa has cooled, add it to the bowl with the vegetables. Toss to combine.
   - Pour the dressing over the salad and toss again to coat everything evenly.
5. **Add Feta (Optional):**
   - If using feta cheese, sprinkle it over the salad and gently toss.
6. **Serve:**
   - Serve immediately or chill in the refrigerator for 30 minutes to let the flavors meld.

Enjoy your vibrant and nutritious Quinoa Salad!

# Cheesy Broccoli Casserole

**Ingredients:**

- 4 cups broccoli florets (fresh or frozen)
- 1 tablespoon olive oil (if using fresh broccoli)
- 1 cup cooked white or brown rice (or 1 can (14.5 oz) of drained canned mushrooms, optional)
- 1 cup shredded cheddar cheese
- 1/2 cup grated Parmesan cheese
- 1/2 cup sour cream
- 1/2 cup mayonnaise
- 1 small onion (chopped)
- 2 cloves garlic (minced)
- 1/2 teaspoon dried thyme (or 1 teaspoon fresh thyme)
- 1/4 teaspoon ground black pepper
- 1/4 teaspoon salt
- 1 cup crushed cornflakes or breadcrumbs (for topping)
- 2 tablespoons butter (for topping)

**Instructions:**

1. **Prepare Broccoli:**
   - If using fresh broccoli, heat olive oil in a large skillet over medium heat. Add broccoli and cook until tender, about 5-7 minutes. If using frozen broccoli, thaw and drain.
2. **Cook Rice (if using):**
   - Cook rice according to package instructions if you haven't done so already. Set aside.
3. **Preheat Oven:**
   - Preheat your oven to 350°F (175°C).
4. **Prepare Casserole Mixture:**
   - In a large bowl, combine the cooked broccoli, rice (or mushrooms), cheddar cheese, Parmesan cheese, sour cream, mayonnaise, chopped onion, minced garlic, thyme, salt, and pepper. Mix well.
5. **Assemble Casserole:**
   - Transfer the broccoli mixture into a greased 9x13-inch baking dish and spread it evenly.
6. **Add Topping:**
   - In a small bowl, mix crushed cornflakes or breadcrumbs with melted butter. Sprinkle this mixture evenly over the top of the casserole.
7. **Bake:**

- Bake in the preheated oven for 25-30 minutes, or until the casserole is bubbly and the topping is golden brown.
8. **Serve:**
    - Let the casserole cool for a few minutes before serving.

Enjoy your creamy, cheesy, and comforting Broccoli Casserole!

**Mediterranean Hummus**

**Ingredients:**

- 1 can (15 oz) chickpeas (drained and rinsed) or 1 1/2 cups cooked chickpeas
- 1/4 cup tahini (sesame paste)
- 1/4 cup extra-virgin olive oil (plus extra for drizzling)
- 2 tablespoons lemon juice (about 1 lemon)
- 2 cloves garlic (minced)
- 1/2 teaspoon ground cumin
- 1/4 teaspoon paprika
- Salt and freshly ground black pepper (to taste)
- 1/4 cup water (more as needed for consistency)
- 1/4 cup Kalamata olives (pitted and sliced, for garnish)
- 1/4 cup cherry tomatoes (halved, for garnish)
- 1/4 cup crumbled feta cheese (optional, for garnish)
- 2 tablespoons chopped fresh parsley (for garnish)

**Instructions:**

1. **Prepare Chickpeas:**
   - If using canned chickpeas, drain and rinse them thoroughly. For a smoother hummus, peel the chickpeas by pinching off the skins (optional).
2. **Blend Ingredients:**
   - In a food processor or blender, combine chickpeas, tahini, olive oil, lemon juice, garlic, cumin, paprika, salt, and pepper.
   - Blend until smooth, adding water a little at a time until you reach your desired consistency. Scrape down the sides as needed.
3. **Taste and Adjust:**
   - Taste the hummus and adjust seasoning if necessary, adding more salt, pepper, or lemon juice as needed.
4. **Serve:**
   - Transfer the hummus to a serving bowl. Garnish with sliced olives, cherry tomatoes, crumbled feta (if using), and chopped parsley.
   - Drizzle a little extra olive oil over the top.
5. **Enjoy:**
   - Serve with pita bread, pita chips, or fresh vegetables for dipping.

Enjoy your fresh and flavorful Mediterranean Hummus!

**Spicy Black Bean Soup**

**Ingredients:**

- 2 tablespoons olive oil
- 1 large onion (chopped)
- 3 cloves garlic (minced)
- 1 bell pepper (red or green, chopped)
- 1-2 jalapeño peppers (seeded and chopped, adjust to heat preference)
- 1 tablespoon ground cumin
- 1 teaspoon smoked paprika
- 1/2 teaspoon chili powder (optional, for extra heat)
- 4 cups vegetable broth (or chicken broth)
- 2 cans (15 oz each) black beans (drained and rinsed) or 3 cups cooked black beans
- 1 can (14.5 oz) diced tomatoes (with juice)
- 1 cup corn kernels (fresh, frozen, or canned)
- Salt and freshly ground black pepper (to taste)
- Juice of 1 lime
- 1/4 cup chopped fresh cilantro (for garnish)

**Optional Toppings:**

- Sour cream or Greek yogurt
- Shredded cheese (cheddar, Monterey Jack, or your choice)
- Sliced avocado
- Tortilla chips
- Chopped green onions

**Instructions:**

1. **Sauté Vegetables:**
   - In a large pot or Dutch oven, heat olive oil over medium heat. Add chopped onion and cook until translucent, about 5 minutes.
   - Add minced garlic, bell pepper, and jalapeño peppers. Cook for another 2-3 minutes until vegetables are tender.
2. **Add Spices:**
   - Stir in ground cumin, smoked paprika, and chili powder (if using). Cook for 1 minute to toast the spices.
3. **Add Broth and Beans:**
   - Pour in the vegetable broth and add the black beans, diced tomatoes (with juice), and corn. Stir to combine.
4. **Simmer Soup:**

- Bring the mixture to a boil, then reduce heat and let it simmer for about 20 minutes to allow flavors to meld. If you prefer a smoother soup, use an immersion blender to blend some or all of the soup, or transfer in batches to a blender.
5. **Season and Finish:**
    - Stir in lime juice and season with salt and pepper to taste.
6. **Serve:**
    - Ladle the soup into bowls and garnish with chopped cilantro and any optional toppings you like.

Enjoy your spicy and flavorful Black Bean Soup!

**Bacon-Wrapped Asparagus**

**Ingredients:**

- 1 bunch of fresh asparagus (about 20-24 spears)
- 10-12 slices of bacon (regular or thick-cut)
- 2 tablespoons olive oil
- Salt and freshly ground black pepper (to taste)
- 1/2 teaspoon garlic powder (optional)
- 1/2 teaspoon smoked paprika (optional)

**Instructions:**

1. **Preheat Oven:**
    - Preheat your oven to 400°F (200°C). Line a baking sheet with parchment paper or aluminum foil for easy cleanup.
2. **Prepare Asparagus:**
    - Trim the woody ends off the asparagus spears. If the spears are very thick, you might want to peel the lower parts with a vegetable peeler for more tenderness.
3. **Wrap Asparagus:**
    - Divide the asparagus into bundles of 4-5 spears each. Take one slice of bacon and wrap it around each bundle of asparagus, starting at one end and spiraling around to the other end. Secure with toothpicks if needed.
4. **Season:**
    - Place the wrapped asparagus bundles on the prepared baking sheet. Brush lightly with olive oil and sprinkle with salt, pepper, garlic powder, and smoked paprika if using.
5. **Bake:**
    - Bake in the preheated oven for 15-20 minutes, or until the bacon is crispy and the asparagus is tender. You may want to flip the bundles halfway through cooking for even crispiness.
6. **Serve:**
    - Remove from the oven and let cool slightly. Serve warm as an appetizer or side dish.

Enjoy your crispy, savory Bacon-Wrapped Asparagus!

## Roasted Butternut Squash Soup

**Ingredients:**

- 1 large butternut squash (peeled, seeded, and cut into cubes)
- 2 tablespoons olive oil
- Salt and freshly ground black pepper (to taste)
- 1 large onion (chopped)
- 2 cloves garlic (minced)
- 1 medium carrot (chopped)
- 1 celery stalk (chopped)
- 4 cups vegetable broth (or chicken broth)
- 1/2 teaspoon ground cumin
- 1/2 teaspoon ground ginger
- 1/4 teaspoon ground nutmeg
- 1/4 teaspoon smoked paprika (optional, for extra depth)
- 1/4 cup heavy cream or coconut milk (optional, for creaminess)
- 1 tablespoon maple syrup or honey (optional, for sweetness)
- Fresh herbs for garnish (such as parsley or thyme, optional)

**Instructions:**

1. **Roast the Squash:**
   - Preheat your oven to 400°F (200°C). Line a baking sheet with parchment paper.
   - Toss the butternut squash cubes with 1 tablespoon of olive oil, salt, and pepper. Spread in a single layer on the baking sheet.
   - Roast for 25-30 minutes, or until the squash is tender and caramelized, turning once halfway through.
2. **Sauté Vegetables:**
   - While the squash is roasting, heat the remaining 1 tablespoon of olive oil in a large pot over medium heat.
   - Add the chopped onion, carrot, and celery. Sauté until the vegetables are softened, about 8-10 minutes.
   - Add minced garlic and cook for an additional 1-2 minutes.
3. **Combine Ingredients:**
   - Once the butternut squash is roasted, add it to the pot with the sautéed vegetables.
   - Pour in the vegetable broth and add the cumin, ginger, nutmeg, and smoked paprika (if using). Bring to a simmer and cook for 10 minutes, allowing flavors to meld.
4. **Blend the Soup:**
   - Use an immersion blender to blend the soup until smooth. Alternatively, you can carefully transfer the soup in batches to a blender and blend until smooth.

5. **Finish and Season:**
    - Stir in the heavy cream or coconut milk if using, and adjust seasoning with additional salt and pepper if needed.
    - If you like a touch of sweetness, add the maple syrup or honey and stir well.
6. **Serve:**
    - Ladle the soup into bowls and garnish with fresh herbs if desired.

Enjoy your creamy and flavorful Roasted Butternut Squash Soup!

www.ingramcontent.com/pod-product-compliance
Lightning Source LLC
LaVergne TN
LVHW081619060526
838201LV00054B/2307